TRUTH, JUSTICE, DIGNITY

ProSe Plaintiff

TERRY

authorHOUSE®

AuthorHouse™
1663 Liberty Drive
Bloomington, IN 47403
www.authorhouse.com
Phone: 1 (800) 839-8640

Published by AuthorHouse 08/16/2019

ISBN: 978-1-7283-2300-8 (sc)
ISBN: 978-1-7283-2299-5 (hc)
ISBN: 978-1-7283-2298-8 (e)

Library of Congress Control Number: 2019911740

Print information available on the last page.

This book is printed on acid-free paper.

Chapter 1

TRUTH, JUSTICE, DIGNITY

Pro Se Plaintiff

This book will inspire anyone to take proper legal action on their own though the courts and become successful in gaining their rights with their employment and their co-worker to include the employer, this book will provide all with a path way for a recourse in its forms, motions, and statue law, to succeed in proving their civil case on their own from submitting a complaint with the equal employment opportunity commission to district court if needed the appeals courts to include the supreme court in Washington D.C. As an author of this book it was written from his insight. Terry was faced with act of un-earn suffering though the action or a ideogy at the hands of another citizen who believed in superior ignorance and Terry also felt he had no way out if at any time you feel this way and it seem to be no way out if it wasn't for people's ego that society place on any citizen reading this book would fine your dignity and lively-hood want be stomped on remember bring legal action by way of the equal employment opportunity commission first where they will grant the right to suit any employer for discrimination from there you begin to regain your dignity and right to prove there is wronged by his employer.

And in this book, you can discover your worth. and a direction to stop unjust and unearned suffering from the hands of your employer and anyone else who bring harm to your dignity and or right as a citizen therefore you should not only get my book you should read it.

Dear readers,

Born in fifty seven, Terry was the seventh son of eleven children, just imagine being raise in the segregated period' remembering being marched outside of elementary school in Texas. All students was instructed to join hands to pray and sing' we shall overcome and then was told Dr. Martin King was not only shot but died' a filing came over Terry he felt not sorrow or anger it was a thought' from listening to dr. king peaching on the fruit of gradulization was where Terry felt sorrow,' he knew things was still going to change once de-segregation was place into law Terry was sent to Jr high where this was a white school' we was assured to be met by a mob of white students and parents, not to exclude administration members we really had to fight anger to get in the school building were we felt we could defend ourselves in a confined area, he felt they did not ask to come nor did they volunteer to be changed from the school closest from our home, (de-segregation) "with a true through piercing his emotions continually he ask himself why should anyone be placed in this kind of anger all they was simply trying to seek an education one of his teacher whom happen to be in a small amount of black teachers he asked why and got a very simply reply' just hold on thing will change, nothing good was ever gained in hearse or the heat of passion, so give the school a chance to get all the education from this experience for your future and other, just know it will be hard but just hang in all will be ok, Terry remembered getting expelled for fighting back a white student who swung at him all he was doing was just defending himself the school administrator gave him a chose he could take five hit with a board with holes or he would leave campass, than the principal called his daddy so he went to the counsel office and called and called his mother by that time his fatter arrived first and from his and my school administrator agreement Terry was supposed to let this white person hit him with that board this thing was about half inch thick with holes in it, his mother told his father that school administrator what she would do with that board she asked the school administrator did he give birth to this black child and told Terry father off his father got him home he tied both of Terry hands together and placed them over the door to beat him if it wasn't for his little sister's and mother this man would as he said he was going to beat Terry to death, you know Terry still love his father from that day till his death and beyond' he couldn't blame him

President Johnson gave way to this sentiment during his speech to congress as he spoke of the unknown, it made me think about Dr. king statements following his words fruit of gradulizion where he told America there will be no business as usual, and Terry reflect on how the south had those die hard Dixie' crats' therefore people didn't know what kind of port they were opening' imagine before Discrimination, humiliation, dignity-stripping third class citizenship horrors this pattern of life for black citizens was demanded and was made to endure, though that port hole it also brought thou it' mental aspect of agreeing saying yes to the white man no matter how wrong he are she was. If Terry could recall soon after his incident with the principal, hitting a student with a board in school became prohibited they legally classified this as corporate punishment, again he gave thought to Ms. smith reply to his question he asked her, than reflected on that day Terry was around the flag post in a since saying goodbye to Dr. King the a few year later a white student though he was trying to talk to his girlfriend he grab Terry and they fell on the ground the school patrol person got Terry off him and man handle to the principal's office he tried to explain the other student grab him and they fell down He said he couldn't stay in the office until school was let out he had to leave the grounds immediately, are he would call the police that he stated that's what he get for beating white boys and was force to walk home thought white territory for ten miles the white boy actually started the fight, he was told by the Jr high school top ranking staff not to put his mind in park because his body need to be with his kind also stated so Terry can beat black boys. He was promoted to the tenth grade he was being sent back to his kind, He was raised in TX. Where the kkk held a meeting at the intercontinental airport and a hotel downtown Clooney the kkk know the black painter party and the black mafia group know of the meeting and the kkk put the word out the grand puba was going to be at the airport but the grand puba was at the hotel where the black mafia was

3

but black painters really wanted the grand puba that why he went to the airport where the kkk members jumping from windows to get away.

In 1974, Terry joined the army at age seventeen where he was faced with not only south hatred there was a twenty four hour of unerupted direct aim of white supremacy to show black soldiers who was in charge and the difference of dignity level be stored on white and black soldier it brought to light what Dr. Martin King was referring in his speech concerning unearned creative suffering this was a common practice of ranking members over squads of soldier where white was a majority it was so bad he wrote to his counsel person after that his company held a meeting on social concerns in his company, he encounter much of dignity stripping attach in 1975 while he was stationed on a military base in 1980. Upon finishing his second tour in the military, Terry return home and was reinstated to his last employment where the manager had an uneasy feeling towards him. He was told on several occasion by the supervisor would express that manager didn't too much like the way how he use those million-dollar words.

Seeds of Injustice

Terry moved to Georgia where he started to work through a temporary company assigned to work for a warehouse company where the majority of the company employee was white female. Although the supervisors and manager was white, he was given distinct educational but distorted history about the north and the south and how the south will rise again' this majority of white people showed the true heritage belief; he had a supervisor tell him with no uncertainty of this vow to the south and he lecture him on how the south will and how he felt the south was going to rise again that was why he participated in any re-enactment of the civil war in 1991 and not long after this episode he was fired.

He remember he was at the company holiday outing. He went to the bathroom where his dinner was on the table as he started to season his food with salt and pepper top was loosen enough and fell off in my food and the whole bottle of salt fell in his plate. There was laughter from the group where he was the only black in the party then jokes passed around the table well he guess it was a joke the secretary and her husband asked him have he ever experienced the windmill. This was an act of sex' the sad thing about this was showing their heritage thought generation of offspring's. They really thought their word actions was just a joke not caring about another citizen dignity, and humanity as to blacks not just an employee; he bought a civil dispute against the company for unlawful termination.

Terry begin working for the county sanitation department it was when he was transferred to the provarizing plaint where again he was subjected to unearned creative suffering by the hands of my white manager. There was a cross in front of his car wrap in a white cloth he took it and showed it to his foreman he laughed and replied are you scarred. Soon after that, he was injured and was placed on light duty where he was directed to shovel cows shit from a feeding belt that feed garbage into a grinding machine. When he told his area director he temporary moved him to the landfill where he was stationed. He had him picking up trash from onside of the road in the ditch where there a dead dog and the dog had a magnet coming out of it than he informed the area director of this and showed him the reason for being on light duty that stated he could not be around bad odors. He replied to finish the task he told him to do or he will be fired. He took as much humiliating suffering just the way of showing their superior being though their method of creative unearned suffering.

Fruits of Gradualism

Terry started to attend Rev. Hosea William meeting on an Ave. In Gallen, where he was seeking assistance for help in bringing the wrong doing that another employer had committed on other black workers and reflected on President Johnson speech as to how the government can pass laws but it was going to take all men to make a change, Rev. William invited him as guest on his program. People crusader show the discussion was based on inequality in the workplace. He attended meeting and met him at the library. In Gallen, where the discussion was based on agreement where a major corporation would agree to reinvest a certain amount of money to the black neighborhood and about the big three one was a high-ranking member on Dr king staff and the two other people was follower of the moment questionable land deal they got est. He made a promise to Rev. William he would not fall into the temptations of the juices of the fruits of gradulizion and agreed that he would continue to carry on his legacy unchained unbought and that he would do all his life and he would give all and do his best to build a law firm in Dove where the elderly and those who need legal help they so needed, he didn't understand why Rev. William family member bought a condo or some type of a real estate around the cascade area if he know Rev. William vision for Dove community and the need of it citizen. This family member had a chance to help others he had a chance to fulfill Rev. William spiritual satisfaction' not forsake others and look out for thou self thus fell for the temptation of the forbidden fruit, not adhering or following the call out from Dr. Martin

King in his message through his have a dream speech where the passage don't bite off the fruit of gradulizion while Rev. William re-enterated to him this was one of the reason Dr. Martin King never ran for any official office because his own conviction, and morale concerns. Other peoples had to agree by signing a pledge not to interfere with the court in their decissioning. That means the only reaction to the court was by a letter to the judge that the court don't even acknowledge Rev. William explain to him why he felt so deeply in his meaning. He was unbought and unchained, as too Dr. King wouldn't run for any office, and the reason why he know how the others had been bought and chained knowing it was the courts where all our gains was won and expressing his dissatisfaction of black official who signed a pledge not to interfere with the court and their uncommon practice in reason and decision making as black was concerned rev. William told him he knew Dr. King teaching was not going to be completely followed because of the selective act of self and not adhering to Dr. King serine warning of the fruit of gradulizion, Rev. William would express joy in stating the best sounds to him was the sound of pit a pat feet's marching for justice, equality and economic freedom. He always told him how his assignment was to go into a town a get the people attention on their issues and report back to Dr. King and a high ranking member, and would always laugh when he ask him why didn't he speak at the match he reply they wasn't going to let him open his mouth up there he was figured to say something crazy and pointed out how they did John Lewis in order to let him go on the stage and make a speech how he considered this was a sign of being bought and chained by the establishment on which they marched for the right to speak their mind as a man, the only thing got them to the point in their quest, Terry first experience In hearing the sound of the pit a pat feet was when he marched with the naacp against police depart top official in the police department for GA. At the time Mr. even was the director for the Glide county, naacp office we was demanding for change in their hiring practice, also the unfair ticketing practice toward black, and the hiring of more black officer to the force.

Terry gained employment with a reproable hotel chain he started as a chief engineer for the hotel chain. There was a white manager who continually tried to get him fired by telling the ranking manager lies. This was madness. Terry was hired instead of this manager spouse this manager would always make up lies, in 2001 he was transferred to another complex as a director of engineer. Terry went on vacation in 2003 and tried to obtain employment at a hotel in Clooney, Texas but was informed by the ranking manager in Clooney Texas they would love to give Terry the job but after talking to the ranking manager in Gallen GA, they was inform there was a assistance general manager posting that the ranking manager guaranteed them Terry would be placed as assistance manager. Once Terry returned from vacation so they didn't want to offer the position to Terry at the Clooney Texas location stating if Terry accept it than down the line Terry feel he cheated himself out of advancing and quit and beginning to state it would be financially suicide and they didn't want to have that burden on their back but upon returning to Gallen GA and return to work. Terry was told by the ranking manager the position was given to another staff member who was not only white they went to the same college the ranking manager attended. He filed a complaint with the equal employment opportunity commission for wage dispute and hiring practice when it was time for bonus compared to the white managers. Terry received less than an third of non-black managers and his department never went over budget even after taking ten percent of engineer budget went to other department to help their line. Terry was told by his manager if something went wrong at the hotel and the general manager or the assistance manager was not there let the sales manager talk to the press or any official reason" college Terry question had she look at his resume it showed proof Terry also attended college,

Friday morning the top official of the company was sitting with friends, Terry a manager and other employees was in the dining room the top official and his friend was laughing he turned around in his chair then told Terry to fix him and his friend some waffles at that time Terry was trying to fix the juice machine. The manager said she would fix the waffles he replied forcibly told Terry. To add insult, Terry was told by another white guests he need to come over to their house and fix their waffle also, [degrading]. Terry was injured he inhaled paint fumes and was directed to get himself and the other engineers to paint the stair wells and four floors that didn't have proper ventilation. Terry was placed on vacation and when it was over, he was placed on short term medical leave. Before this long term leave over he was fired then his claim at the EEOC for wrongful termination. While he was out on long term medical leave, he was informed he had two years to return to duty, by the company insurer. For some reason unknown, he was terminated. He filed a complaint with the EEOC for wrongful termination he was given the right to sue he filed a suit with the federal court and was granted the right to proceed his first and only attorney insist he release them one week before a vidle motion was to be filed in court this motion if it was not filed on time the district court would have thrown out' his civil case on default and Terry would have lost on default, the attorney call him to the office he thought his motion was ready to be signed to send to be placed on docket, instead when the legal personal came into the room the first words was you have to release me, Terry was unaware of what was really going on, he responded what was she talking about. She then stated she just talked to the opposing counsel and just can't represent him. He asked the attorney why again she replied she has been told, and then stated before Terry left out the door he was not and will not be releasing them from his civil case. The attorney put the paperwork on the table and started taking the pin from the bob that held the hair down it was in a ball once the attorney walked in the conference room stating Terry had to release them from representing him he tried to informed of the attorney the importance of having the motion filed with in less than a week and then unloosen the top button of the blouse. Terry replied let me see the papers as he was looking at the papers he was slowly moving to the door after opening the door where the secretary could hear what was going on in the room, Terry thawed the papers back on the table and ran out the door pass the secretary could see his close was not wrinkled then Terry went to another lawyer to seek assistance. He informed Terry that he knew his last attorney then sent Terry out the room and called the attorney. He called Terry back in and inform him the attorney told him something disturbing and if got out she would be disbarred even might get jail time, for whatever the other attorneys used to get her not to represents him in fact the district judge order Terry attorney to represents him, ordering that the only way the attorney could be release by the court from Terry civil case where the firm was ordered to complete a list of demands to the best Terry knowledge ten criterial that was to be performed before the court would release them from representing counsel to my civil case the order was not obeyed, Terry represents himself as a pro se plaintiff, during an deposition the opposing counsel told Terry they didn't break no ethic rules than stated your former attorney did so.two administrators was contradicting their own ruling and so was one stated to the appeals court Terry was trying to tell them how to do their job in words to that affect, he enter a motion requesting the opposing attorney not be able to represents the civil case, because of a conflict of interest, to no prevail, there was no motion filed by opposing attorney after the legally filing dates, there was more than two motion before the court was aware whom the opposing counsel for the civil case in front of the court this was out of nature and unconstitutional, the administrator ordered the opposing attorney to respond to a motion entered on docket the opposing attorney told the judge no they hadn't respond and the firm was not intending to respond the administrator ordered the attorney to respond, this was on a conference call between Terry the administrator and the opposing attorney' the response was not ever entered, to the court, after being ordered by the administrator alone should have placed the attorneys in default, this call was in the administrator chambers, Terry felt it should have been recorded because it meeting was of legal matters, where a ruling was made, he remembered filing a motion for intervention on the district court finding, by the administrator's rationing the federal court law clerk assigned the motion that filed to the same administrator hand Terry was requesting for intervention on ruling and objective reasoning

The administrator's allowed opposing counsel to enter a list of motions and response that was untrue on its nature than ruled in favor of the opposing attorney hear-say motions, and deny some of Terry responds as hear-say some would agree the only thing he received was true injustice and some will say the rule of law was not served, some ask when is it true justice, why did the one administrator defied the other administrator ruling and gave the defendants, a path to a unjust earning of justice some may ask what would have an administrator to make a statement to the appeals court stating a Pro Se plaintiff meaning Terry)" want the court to change its normal way of during its business' it made me reflect on the path age from Dr. King stating telling America in 1968 there will be no business as usual as so stated by the district judge his words to the court of appeals[Terry think we are to change the way we have been doing business] all must insist the court is not a business it is place for justice by the law and the constitution from which the founding fathers set to follow]. also, I reflected on Rev. William dissatisfied in not being able to speak his words as he did when they were on their quest there was signs being carried stating I AM A MAN. This should've included the right to express your likes and dis-likes. this didn't only present itself in the district court, it reared it unconstitutional head in the eleventh circuit of appeal court, and the U.S. Supreme court, Terry presented his case as a pro se plaintiff, [a person whom plead their civil case on their own] some may express the inequality in the courts' but I would sermit to all of those who are standing on the threshold which lead into the palace of justice, being wronged, humiliated and striped of your dignity remember this is not in the constitution, and neither palace of justice decisions should not be regarded as business as usual in the courts be it the district court appeals court to include the supreme court,

No, Terry didn't received the truth-dignity and justice under the constitution for an American citizen whom been wronged, The district court changed Terry complaint to satisfy their need for business and the eleventh circuit court of appeals refuse to review Terry initial entry to the district court for proper ruling not to exclude the magistrate judge declared the hotel chain was found in default, but the district judge rejected the magistrate judge recommendation same action received from the eleventh circuit court of appeals to include the U.S Supreme COURT. In Washington D.C. Terry initial and original complaint to the equal employment opportunity commission was termination while on long term company medical leave not as the district court so made changed to his complaint expressing Terry complaint was based on me being out on a family medical leave act. [FMLA] not so: his initial claim to the court has not been judicated to this day. To add he don't and will not ever think the building that house the lady of liberty where truth, justice and dignity is to set forth for all citizens shouldn't be a business somewhere we was told and read when you walk thou them doors down those hallways to a court room to seek justice you are not walking down a hallway to a boardroom NOOO! This building is not a building designed for executive's with corporate plain or agenda this building the court house is designed by the constitution under the rules of BY and for the people in this building is set in place with citizens as fact finders of justice and fairness for her citizens not as an executives business this is why people's feel a understanding of Dr Martin King words stating to the white power structure there be will no business as usual tomorrow.

Just imagine you would start your concern hoping the board understand the critical stage in the black citizen struggle, to graph justice for all citizen, you would be asking their office for assistance to bring a close to any bias and setbacks in so far as you bring a civil case that would place you as a plaintiff you are asking a chance for gaining your rights to seek justice and fairness in the workplace also in the judicial system for all citizen, in your submission of concern should be addressing judges performing their legal duties as an arbitrator into racial concern against corporations and their misdeeds.

Just imagine filing a complaint to the judicial review board with concerns on judges showing bias in their reasoning to include your concern about their official capacity as arbitrator than amageing the board reply back stating they didn't handle such claim you refer for their assistance., I would re-submit there are constitutional facts their office understanding the hard ship was added to your legal issue's by the judge's placed on black citizen in their hopes when using bias rational when all they was trying to prove misdeeds and unequal practice of employers and the courts, always introduce the misdeeds of the courts and how it's hard enough trying To proving misdeeds on employers, and the courts and how it makes it hard for any citizen to understand the true meaning of the fable the true meaning of the legal beckon of the Northern Judicial freedom and right to a path to a fair and equal trail

Just imagine the arbitrators allowed the defendant to change your filing from what you entered, the arbitrators allowed the defendant to file a motion to the court that was based on non-factual statement with no supporting facts, express the court ruled in favor of defendants hear-say motion,. One would wonder is this the way business done. In a place where judicial standing is adhered though to give true justice is supporting to work for citizen.

Chapter II

PROCEED TO JUSTICE

Disclaimer

As the author of this book, Terry is not a lawyer but he is good standing in the court system within sight on a civil law-suit entered against a former employer. That proceeded though the equal employment opportunity commission investigation where Terry gained the right to sue, proceeding he entered a lawsuit into the federal district court for the northern district. Then entered though eleventh circuit court of appeals. There he not only entered the eleventh circuit court of appeals, to include he entered a filing in the U.S. Supreme Court as a pro se plaintiff. Terry was granted the right to appeal his civil case in the United States Supreme Court of Appeal to be headed.

Defendant No. 3
    Name
    Job or Title *(if known)*
    Address

	City	State	Zip Code

    County
    Telephone Number
    E-Mail Address *(if known)*

☐ Individual capacity   ☐ Official capacity

Defendant No. 4
    Name
    Job or Title *(if known)*
    Address

	City	State	Zip Code

    County
    Telephone Number
    E-Mail Address *(if known)*

☐ Individual capacity   ☐ Official capacity

II.   Basis for Jurisdiction

Under 42 U.S.C. § 1983, you may sue state or local officials for the "deprivation of any rights, privileges, or immunities secured by the Constitution and [federal laws]." Under *Bivens v. Six Unknown Named Agents of Federal Bureau of Narcotics, 403 U.S. 388 (1971)*, you may sue federal officials for the violation of certain constitutional rights.

A.   Are you bringing suit against *(check all that apply)*:

    ☐ Federal officials (a *Bivens* claim)

    ☐ State or local officials (a § 1983 claim)

B.   Section 1983 allows claims alleging the "deprivation of any rights, privileges, or immunities secured by the Constitution and [federal laws]." 42 U.S.C. § 1983. If you are suing under section 1983, what federal constitutional or statutory right(s) do you claim is/are being violated by state or local officials?

C.   Plaintiffs suing under *Bivens* may only recover for the violation of certain constitutional rights. If you are suing under *Bivens*, what constitutional right(s) do you claim is/are being violated by federal officials?

19

D. Section 1983 allows defendants to be found liable only when they have acted "under color of any statute, ordinance, regulation, custom, or usage, of any State or Territory or the District of Columbia." 42 U.S.C. § 1983. If you are suing under section 1983, explain how each defendant acted under color of state or local law. If you are suing under *Bivens*, explain how each defendant acted under color of federal law. Attach additional pages if needed.

III. Statement of Claim

State as briefly as possible the facts of your case. Describe how each defendant was personally involved in the alleged wrongful action, along with the dates and locations of all relevant events. You may wish to include further details such as the names of other persons involved in the events giving rise to your claims. Do not cite any cases or statutes. If more than one claim is asserted, number each claim and write a short and plain statement of each claim in a separate paragraph. Attach additional pages if needed.

A. Where did the events giving rise to your claim(s) occur?

B. What date and approximate time did the events giving rise to your claim(s) occur?

C. What are the facts underlying your claim(s)? *(For example: What happened to you? Who did what? Was anyone else involved? Who else saw what happened?)*

21

IV.   **Injuries**

If you sustained injuries related to the events alleged above, describe your injuries and state what medical treatment, if any, you required and did or did not receive.

V.   **Relief**

State briefly what you want the court to do for you. Make no legal arguments. Do not cite any cases or statutes. If requesting money damages, include the amounts of any actual damages and/or punitive damages claimed for the acts alleged. Explain the basis for these claims.

VI.   Certification and Closing

Under Federal Rule of Civil Procedure 11, by signing below, I certify to the best of my knowledge, information, and belief that this complaint: (1) is not being presented for an improper purpose, such as to harass, cause unnecessary delay, or needlessly increase the cost of litigation; (2) is supported by existing law or by a nonfrivolous argument for extending, modifying, or reversing existing law; (3) the factual contentions have evidentiary support or, if specifically so identified, will likely have evidentiary support after a reasonable opportunity for further investigation or discovery; and (4) the complaint otherwise complies with the requirements of Rule 11.

A.   For Parties Without an Attorney

I agree to provide the Clerk's Office with any changes to my address where case–related papers may be served. I understand that my failure to keep a current address on file with the Clerk's Office may result in the dismissal of my case.

Date of signing:

Signature of Plaintiff

Printed Name of Plaintiff

B.   For Attorneys

Date of signing:

Signature of Attorney

Printed Name of Attorney

Bar Number

Name of Law Firm

Address

	City	State	Zip Code

Telephone Number

E-mail Address

25

APPENDIX OF FORMS

Form 1. **Notice of Appeal to a Court of Appeals From a Judgment or Order of a District Court**

United States District Court for the _____

District of _____

File Number _____

A. B., Plaintiff

        v.   Notice of Appeal

C. D., Defendant

Notice is hereby given that __(here name all parties taking the appeal)__, (plaintiffs) (defendants) in the above named case,* hereby appeal to the United States Court of Appeals for the _____ Circuit (from the final judgment) (from an order (describing it)) entered in this action on the ____ day of _____ 20__

(s) _____

_____ _____ _____

Address: _____

[*Note to inmate filers*: If you are an inmate confined in an institution and you seek the timing benefit

along with this Notice of Appeal.]

See Rule 3(c) for permissible ways of identifying appellants.

Dec. 1, 2016.)

CONCLUSION

The petition for a writ of certiorari should be granted.

      Respectfully submitted,

      _____

      Date: _____

No. _____

_____

IN THE

SUPREME COURT OF THE UNITED STATES

_____

_____ — PETITIONER
(Your Name)

VS.

_____ — RESPONDENT(S)

PROOF OF SERVICE

I, _____, do swear or declare that on this date,
_____, 20___, as required by Supreme Court Rule 29 I have
served the enclosed MOTION FOR LEAVE TO PROCEED *IN FORMA PAUPERIS*
and PETITION FOR A WRIT OF CERTIORARI on each party to the above proceeding
or that party's counsel, and on every other person required to be served, by depositing
an envelope containing the above documents in the United States mail properly addressed
to each of them and with first-class postage prepaid, or by delivery to a third-party
commercial carrier for delivery within 3 calendar days.

The names and addresses of those served are as follows:

_____

_____

_____

I declare under penalty of perjury that the foregoing is true and correct.

Executed on _____, 20___

_____
(Signature)

31

UNITED STATES DISTRICT COURT
NORTHERN DISTRICT OF *G.A.*
PRO SE APPLICANT ELECTRONIC FILING REGISTRATION FORM

This form is used to register for an account on the Northern District of Ohio Electronic Filing System (the system). Registered pro se applicants will have privileges to electronically submit documents in a particular case and to view the electronic docket sheets and documents. By registering, pro se applicants consent to receiving electronic notice of filings through the system. The following information is required for registration:

PLEASE TYPE

Mr. / Mrs. / Ms. (circle one)

First Name: _____   Middle Name: _____

Last Name: _____   If appropriate circle one: Senior / Junior / II / III

Address: _____

_____

City: _____   State: _____   Zip Code: _____

Voice Telephone Number: (_____) _____   Fax Number: (_____) _____

Internet Mail Address: _____

Pro se applicants seeking to file documents electronically must be granted permission by the Judicial Officer to register and file documents electronically in a particular case pursuant to LR 5.1 and LCrR 49.2

Date permission granted to register & file documents electronically: _____ in case number: _____

By submitting this registration form, the undersigned agrees to abide by all Court rules, orders and policies and procedures governing the use of the electronic filing system. The undersigned understands that notice of filings will be received via the Court's electronic filing system. The combination of user id and password will serve as the signature of the pro se litigant filing the document(s). Users must protect the security of their passwords and immediately notify the Court if they learn that their password has been compromised by an unauthorized user.

_____   _____
Signature of Pro Se Applicant   Date

Submit completed Registration Form to: Sandy Opacich, Clerk
United States District Court
Attention: Electronic Filing System Registration
801 West Superior Avenue
Cleveland, OH 44113-1830

Once your registration is complete, you will receive notification by email as to your user id and password needed to access the system. Procedures for using the system will be available for downloading when you access the system via the Internet. You may contact the Electronic Filing Help Desk in the Clerk's Office at 1-800-355-8498 if you have any questions concerning the registration process or the use of the electronic filing system.

****

The CM/ECF system also requires users to have a separate PACER id and password in order to view documents in the CM/ECF system. PACER accounts can be established through the PACER Service Center:

PACER Service Center
P.O. Box 780549
San Antonio, TX 78278
800-676-6856

For further information on the support services provided by the PACER Service Center, please visit the PACER website at www.pacer.psc.uscourts.gov

For your information, the Judicial Conference of the United States has established a fee to be collected for access to PACER. All registered individuals will be charged a user fee. Please refer to the PACER Service Center regarding fees.

AO 432
(Rev. 2/84)

Administrative Office of the United States Courts

WITNESS AND EXHIBIT RECORD

DATE	CASE NUMBER	OPERATOR			PAGE NUMBER	
NAME OF WITNESS		DIRECT	CROSS	REDIRECT	RECROSS	PRESIDING OFFICIAL

EXHIBIT NUMBER	DESCRIPTION	ID	ADMITTED IN EVIDENCE

The JS 44 civil cover sheet and the information contained herein neither replace nor supplement the filing and service of pleadings or other papers as required by law, except as provided by local rules of court. This form, approved by the Judicial Conference of the United States in September 1974, is required for the use of the Clerk of Court for the purpose of initiating the civil docket sheet. *(SEE INSTRUCTIONS ON NEXT PAGE OF THIS FORM.)*

I. (a) PLAINTIFFS

DEFENDANTS

(b) County of Residence of First Listed Plaintiff _____
(EXCEPT IN U.S. PLAINTIFF CASES)

County of Residence of First Listed Defendant _____
(IN U.S. PLAINTIFF CASES ONLY)
NOTE: IN LAND CONDEMNATION CASES, USE THE LOCATION OF
THE TRACT OF LAND INVOLVED.

(c) Attorneys *(Firm Name, Address, and Telephone Number)*

Attorneys *(If Known)*

II. BASIS OF JURISDICTION *(Place an "X" in One Box Only)*

- ☐ 1 U.S. Government Plaintiff
- ☐ 3 Federal Question *(U.S. Government Not a Party)*
- ☐ 2 U.S. Government Defendant
- ☐ 4 Diversity *(Indicate Citizenship of Parties in Item III)*

III. CITIZENSHIP OF PRINCIPAL PARTIES *(Place an "X" in One Box for Plaintiff and One Box for Defendant)*
(For Diversity Cases Only)

	PTF	DEF		PTF	DEF
Citizen of This State	☐ 1	☐ 1	Incorporated or Principal Place of Business In This State	☐ 4	☐ 4
Citizen of Another State	☐ 2	☐ 2	Incorporated and Principal Place of Business In Another State	☐ 5	☐ 5
Citizen or Subject of a Foreign Country	☐ 3	☐ 3	Foreign Nation	☐ 6	☐ 6

IV. NATURE OF SUIT *(Place an "X" in One Box Only)*

Click here for: Nature of Suit Code Descriptions.

CONTRACT	TORTS		FORFEITURE/PENALTY	BANKRUPTCY	OTHER STATUTES
☐ 110 Insurance	**PERSONAL INJURY**	**PERSONAL INJURY**	☐ 625 Drug Related Seizure of Property 21 USC 881	☐ 422 Appeal 28 USC 158	☐ 375 False Claims Act
☐ 120 Marine	☐ 310 Airplane	☐ 365 Personal Injury - Product Liability	☐ 690 Other	☐ 423 Withdrawal 28 USC 157	☐ 376 Qui Tam (31 USC 3729(a))
☐ 130 Miller Act	☐ 315 Airplane Product Liability	☐ 367 Health Care/ Pharmaceutical Personal Injury Product Liability			☐ 400 State Reapportionment
☐ 140 Negotiable Instrument	☐ 320 Assault, Libel & Slander			**PROPERTY RIGHTS**	☐ 410 Antitrust
☐ 150 Recovery of Overpayment & Enforcement of Judgment	☐ 330 Federal Employers' Liability	☐ 368 Asbestos Personal Injury Product Liability		☐ 820 Copyrights	☐ 430 Banks and Banking
☐ 151 Medicare Act	☐ 340 Marine			☐ 830 Patent	☐ 450 Commerce
☐ 152 Recovery of Defaulted Student Loans (Excludes Veterans)	☐ 345 Marine Product Liability	**PERSONAL PROPERTY**		☐ 835 Patent - Abbreviated New Drug Application	☐ 460 Deportation
☐ 153 Recovery of Overpayment of Veteran's Benefits	☐ 350 Motor Vehicle	☐ 370 Other Fraud	**LABOR**	☐ 840 Trademark	☐ 470 Racketeer Influenced and Corrupt Organizations
☐ 160 Stockholders' Suits	☐ 355 Motor Vehicle Product Liability	☐ 371 Truth in Lending	☐ 710 Fair Labor Standards Act	**SOCIAL SECURITY**	☐ 480 Consumer Credit
☐ 190 Other Contract	☐ 360 Other Personal Injury	☐ 380 Other Personal Property Damage	☐ 720 Labor/Management Relations	☐ 861 HIA (1395ff)	☐ 485 Telephone Consumer Protection Act
☐ 195 Contract Product Liability	☐ 362 Personal Injury - Medical Malpractice	☐ 385 Property Damage Product Liability	☐ 740 Railway Labor Act	☐ 862 Black Lung (923)	☐ 490 Cable/Sat TV
☐ 196 Franchise			☐ 751 Family and Medical Leave Act	☐ 863 DIWC/DIWW (405(g))	☐ 850 Securities/Commodities/ Exchange
				☐ 864 SSID Title XVI	☐ 890 Other Statutory Actions
REAL PROPERTY	**CIVIL RIGHTS**	**PRISONER PETITIONS**	☐ 790 Other Labor Litigation	☐ 865 RSI (405(g))	☐ 891 Agricultural Acts
☐ 210 Land Condemnation	☐ 440 Other Civil Rights	**Habeas Corpus:**	☐ 791 Employee Retirement Income Security Act		☐ 893 Environmental Matters
☐ 220 Foreclosure	☐ 441 Voting	☐ 463 Alien Detainee		**FEDERAL TAX SUITS**	☐ 895 Freedom of Information Act
☐ 230 Rent Lease & Ejectment	☐ 442 Employment	☐ 510 Motions to Vacate Sentence		☐ 870 Taxes (U.S. Plaintiff or Defendant)	☐ 896 Arbitration
☐ 240 Torts to Land	☐ 443 Housing/ Accommodations	☐ 530 General		☐ 871 IRS—Third Party 26 USC 7609	☐ 899 Administrative Procedure Act/Review or Appeal of Agency Decision
☐ 245 Tort Product Liability	☐ 445 Amer. w/Disabilities - Employment	☐ 535 Death Penalty	**IMMIGRATION**		☐ 950 Constitutionality of State Statutes
☐ 290 All Other Real Property	☐ 446 Amer. w/Disabilities - Other	**Other:**	☐ 462 Naturalization Application		
	☐ 448 Education	☐ 540 Mandamus & Other	☐ 465 Other Immigration Actions		
		☐ 550 Civil Rights			
		☐ 555 Prison Condition			
		☐ 560 Civil Detainee - Conditions of Confinement			

V. ORIGIN *(Place an "X" in One Box Only)*

- ☐ 1 Original Proceeding
- ☐ 2 Removed from State Court
- ☐ 3 Remanded from Appellate Court
- ☐ 4 Reinstated or Reopened
- ☐ 5 Transferred from Another District *(specify)*
- ☐ 6 Multidistrict Litigation - Transfer
- ☐ 8 Multidistrict Litigation - Direct File

VI. CAUSE OF ACTION

Cite the U.S. Civil Statute under which you are filing *(Do not cite jurisdictional statutes unless diversity)*:

Brief description of cause:

VII. REQUESTED IN COMPLAINT:

☐ CHECK IF THIS IS A CLASS ACTION UNDER RULE 23, F.R.Cv.P.

DEMAND $

CHECK YES only if demanded in complaint:
JURY DEMAND: ☐ Yes ☐ No

VIII. RELATED CASE(S) IF ANY

(See instructions)

JUDGE _____

DOCKET NUMBER _____

DATE _____

SIGNATURE OF ATTORNEY OF RECORD _____

IN THE UNITED STATES DISTRICT COURT
FOR THE NORTHERN DISTRICT OF *GA.*

(Fill in the name) ,	))))	
Plaintiff	))	CASE NO. (Leave blank)
-vs-	))))	JUDGE (Leave blank)
(Fill in the name/names) ,	)))	COMPLAINT
Defendant(s)	))	

In numbered paragraphs, and using as many pages as you need:

- Name the parties and give their addresses.

- State the basis of the court's jurisdiction (e.g.: 42 U.S.C. § 1983 – Civil Rights; 42 U.S.C. § 2000e – Title VII – Discrimination).

- Then simply tell the facts of your case, including names, dates, etc.

- Finally, ask the court for whatever relief you desire (e.g., injunction, money damages, etc.)

At the end of the complaint, sign your name. Underneath the signature print your name and address. Date the document.

O:\Pro Se Forms\Complaint Sample..wpd

IN THE UNITED STATES DISTRICT COURT
FOR THE NORTHERN DISTRICT OF OHIO

_____, Plaintiff -vs- _____, Defendant(s)	))))) CASE NO._____))) JUDGE _____)))) COMPLAINT))

Pro Se IFP Complaint Instructions

Documents Needed for Filing

1. **Application to Proceed without Prepaying Fees or Costs (In Forma Pauperis - IFP) - AO 240**

2. **Civil Cover Sheet** (2 stapled pages)

3. **Complaint** (see sample)

   * You will need the original plus, one copy for each defendant, one copy for each of the U.S. Attorneys (if applicable), and a copy for yourself.

4. **Summonses** (2 for each named defendant)(see sample)

   * if a U.S. Government agency or officer is sued, you must also provide summonses for the U.S. Attorney General (Dept. of Justice, Washington, D.C. 20044) and the U.S. Attorney, N.D. Ohio (801 West Superior Avenue, Suite 400, Cleveland, Ohio 44113-1852).

5. **U.S. Marshal Forms** (1 for each named defendant)(see sample)

   * if a U.S. Government agency or officer is sued, you must also provide U.S. Marshal Forms for the U.S. Attorney General and the local U.S. Attorney.

Procedure for Filing

1. File all of the above by mailing it to the court or by bringing it personally.

2. The court will decide whether to grant your IFP and will notify you of its decision by means of a signed order. (Note: if it is denied, your case will not proceed unless you pay the $400 filing fee.)

3. If you are granted IFP status, your complaint will be reviewed by a judge to determine if it must be dismissed pursuant to 28 U.S.C. § 1915. If it is dismissed, you will be notified by means of a signed order from the judge stating the reasons for dismissal.

4. If the case is not dismissed, the U.S. Marshal will be directed to serve the defendant(s) with the summons(es) and your complaint. The defendant(s) will be directed to respond your complaint and serve you with a copy of the response.

UNITED STATES DISTRICT COURT
Northern District of $G A$.

_____	CONSENT TO EXERCISE OF JURISDICTION
Plaintiff	BY A UNITED STATES MAGISTRATE JUDGE
v.	AND ORDER OF REFERENCE
_____	Case Number: _____
Defendant	

CONSENT TO EXERCISE OF JURISDICTION BY A UNITED STATES MAGISTRATE JUDGE

In accordance with the provisions of 28 U.S.C. 636(c) and Fed. R. Civ. P. 73, the parties in this case hereby voluntarily consent to have a United States magistrate judge conduct any and all further proceedings in the case, including the trial, and order the entry of a final judgment.

Signatures	Party Represented	Date
_____	_____	_____
_____	_____	_____
_____	_____	_____
_____	_____	_____
_____	_____	_____
_____	_____	_____

ORDER OF REFERENCE

IT IS HEREBY ORDERED that this case be referred to _____United States Magistrate Judge, for all further proceedings and the entry of judgment in accordance with 28 U.S. C. 636(c), Fed.R.Civ.P. 73 and the foregoing consent of the parties.

_____   _____
Date   _United States District Judge_

NOTE: RETURN THIS FORM TO THE CLERK OF THE COURT **_ONLY IF_** ALL PARTIES
                   HAVE CONSENTED **_ON THIS FORM_** TO THE EXERCISE OF JURISDICTION BY
                   A UNITED STATES MAGISTRATE JUDGE.

47

UNITED STATES DISTRICT COURT
for the

_____)	
Plaintiff)	
v.)	Civil Action No.
_____)	
Defendant)	

SUBPOENA TO APPEAR AND TESTIFY
AT A HEARING OR TRIAL IN A CIVIL ACTION

To:

YOU ARE COMMANDED to appear in the United States district court at the time, date, and place set forth below to testify at a hearing or trial in this civil action. When you arrive, you must remain at the court until the judge or a court officer allows you to leave. If you are an organization that is *not* a party in this case, you must designate one or more officers, directors, or managing agents, or designate other persons who consent to testify on your behalf about the following matters, or those set forth in an attachment:

Place:	Courtroom No.:
	Date and Time:

You must also bring with you the following documents, electronically stored information, or objects *(blank if not applicable)*:

The provisions of Fed. R. Civ. P. 45(c), relating to your protection as a person subject to a subpoena, and Fed. R. Civ. P. 45 (d) and (e), relating to your duty to respond to this subpoena and the potential consequences of not doing so, are attached.

Date: _____

SANDY OPACICH, CLERK OF COURT

OR

_____   _____
Signature of Clerk or Deputy Clerk   *Attorney's signature*

The name, address, e-mail, and telephone number of the attorney representing *(name of party)* _____
_____ , who issues or requests this subpoena, are:

Civil Action No.

PROOF OF SERVICE
(This section should not be filed with the court unless required by Fed. R. Civ. P. 45.)

This subpoena for *(name of individual and title, if any)* _____

was received by me on *(date)* _____ .

□ I served the subpoena by delivering a copy to the named person as follows: _____

_____

_____ on *(date)* _____ ; or

□ I returned the subpoena unexecuted because: _____

_____

Unless the subpoena was issued on behalf of the United States, or one of its officers or agents, I have also tendered to the witness fees for one day's attendance, and the mileage allowed by law, in the amount of

$ _____ .

My fees are $ _____ for travel and $ _____ for services, for a total of $ 0.00

I declare under penalty of perjury that this information is true.

Date: _____

_____
Server's signature

_____
Printed name and title

_____
Server's address

Additional information regarding attempted service, etc:

Civil Pro Se Forms

Form Number	Form Name	Category
Pro Se 1	Complaint for a Civil Case	Civil Pro Se Forms
Pro Se 2	Complaint and Request for Injunction	Civil Pro Se Forms
Pro Se 3	Defendant's Answer to the Complaint	Civil Pro Se Forms
Pro Se 4	Complaint for a Civil Case Alleging Breach of Contract	Civil Pro Se Forms
Pro Se 5	Complaint for a Civil Case Alleging Negligence	Civil Pro Se Forms
Pro Se 6	Complaint for a Civil Case Alleging that the Defendant Owes the Plaintiff a Sum of Money	Civil Pro Se Forms
Pro Se 7	Complaint for Employment Discrimination	Civil Pro Se Forms
Pro Se 8	Complaint for Violations of Fair Labor Standards	Civil Pro Se Forms
Pro Se 9	Complaint for Specific Performance or Damages Based on a Contract to Convey Real Property	Civil Pro Se Forms
Pro Se 10	Complaint for the Conversion of Property	Civil Pro Se Forms
Pro Se 11	Third Party Complaint	Civil Pro Se Forms
Pro Se 12	Complaint for Interpleader and Declaratory Relief	Civil Pro Se Forms
Pro Se 13	Complaint for Review of Social Security Decision	Civil Pro Se Forms
Pro Se 14	Complaint for Violation of Civil Rights (Prisoner)	Civil Pro Se Forms
Pro Se 15	Complaint for Violation of Civil Rights (Non-Prisoner)	Civil Pro Se Forms

Forms for review in pro se filing

Complaint for violation of fair labor standards

Complaint for employment discrimination

Complaint for a civil case

Summons in a civil case

Consent to exercise of jurisdiction by a united states magistrate judge

Subpoena to appear and testify at a hearing or in a trail in a civil action

Enter complaint in the district court (ga. And ohio servs as same)

Pro se complaint instructions

Civil pro se forms

Pro se applicant electronic filing registration form

Witness and exhibit record

Civil cover sheet

Notice of a lawsuit and request to waive service of a summons

Application to proceed in district court without prepaying fees and costs

Complaint for violation of civil rights

Copy of docketing form

Notice of appeal to a court of appeals from judgment or order of a district court

indigent petitioners for writ of certiorari in the supreme court

13.3. Filing in the Supreme Court means the actual receipt of documents by the Clerk; or their deposit in the United States mail, with first-class postage prepaid, on or before the final date allowed for filing; or their delivery to a third-party commercial carrier, on or before the final date allowed for filing, for delivery to the Clerk within 3 calendar days. See Rule 29.2.

IV. What To File

Unless you are an inmate confined in an institution and not represented by counsel, file:

—An original and ten copies of a motion for leave to proceed *in forma pauperis* and an original and 10 copies of an affidavit or declaration in support thereof. See Rule 39.

—An original and 10 copies of a petition for a writ of certiorari with an appendix consisting of a copy of the judgment or decree you are asking this Court to review including any order on rehearing, and copies of any opinions or orders by any courts or administrative agencies that have previously considered your case. See Rule 14.1(i).

—One affidavit or declaration showing that all opposing parties or their counsel have been served with a copy of the papers filed in this Court. See Rule 29.

If you are an inmate confined in an institution and not represented by counsel, you need file only the original of the motion for leave to proceed *in forma pauperis*, affidavit or declaration in support of the motion for leave to proceed *in forma pauperis*, the petition for a writ of certiorari, and proof of service.

The attached forms may be used for the original motion, affidavit or declaration, and petition, and should be stapled together in that order. The proof of service should be included as a detached sheet, and the form provided may be used.

V. Page Limitation

The petition for a writ of certiorari may not exceed 40 pages excluding the pages that precede Page 1 of the form. The documents required to be contained in the appendix to the petition do not count toward the page limit. See Rule 33.2(b).

VI. Method of Filing

All documents to be filed in this Court must be addressed to the Clerk, Supreme Court of the United States, Washington, D. C. 20543 and must be served on opposing parties or their counsel in accordance with Rule 29.

INSTRUCTIONS FOR COMPLETING FORMS

I.   Motion for Leave to Proceed *In Forma Pauperis* - Rule 39

A.. On the form provided for the motion for leave to proceed *in forma pauperis*, leave the case number blank. The number will be assigned by the Clerk when the case is docketed.

B. On the line in the case caption for "petitioner", type your name. As a *pro se* petitioner, you may represent only yourself. On the line for "respondent", type the name of the opposing party in the lower court. If there are multiple respondents, enter the first respondent, as the name appeared on the lower court decision, followed by "et al." to indicate that there are other respondents. The additional parties must be listed in the LIST OF PARTIES section of the petition.

C. If the lower courts in your case granted you leave to proceed *in forma pauperis*, check the appropriate space and indicate the court or courts that allowed you to proceed *in forma pauperis*. If none of the lower courts granted you leave to proceed *in forma pauperis*, check the block that so indicates.

D. Sign the motion on the signature line.

II.   Affidavit or Declaration in Support of Motion for Leave to Proceed *In Forma Pauperis*

On the form provided, answer fully each of the questions. If the answer to a question is "0," "none," or "not applicable (N/A)," enter that response. If you need more space to answer a question or to explain your answer, attach a separate sheet of paper, identified with your name and the question number. Unless each question is fully answered, the Clerk will not accept the petition. The form must either be notarized or be in the form of a declaration. See 28 U. S. C. § 1746.

III.   Cover Page - Rule 34

When you complete the form for the cover page:

A. Leave case number blank. The number will be assigned by the Clerk when the case is docketed.

B. Complete the case caption as you did on the motion for leave to proceed *in forma pauperis*.

C. List the court from which the action is brought on the line following the words "on petition for a writ of certiorari to." If your case is from a state court, enter the name of the court that last addressed the merits of the case. For example, if the highest state court denied discretionary review, and the state court of appeals affirmed the decision of the trial court, the state court of appeals should be listed. If your case is federal, the United States court of

OFFICE OF THE CLERK
SUPREME COURT OF THE UNITED STATES
WASHINGTON, D. C. 20543

GUIDE FOR PROSPECTIVE INDIGENT PETITIONERS FOR WRITS OF CERTIORARI

I. Introduction

These instructions and forms are designed to assist petitioners who are proceeding *in forma pauperis* and without the assistance of counsel. A copy of the Rules of the Supreme Court, which establish the procedures that must be followed, is also enclosed. Be sure to read the following Rules carefully:

Rules 10-14 (Petitioning for certiorari)
Rule 29 (Filing and service on opposing party or counsel)
Rule 30 (Computation and extension of time)
Rules 33.2 and 34 (Preparing pleadings on 8½ x 11 inch paper)
Rule 39 (Proceedings *in forma pauperis*)

II. Nature of Supreme Court Review

It is important to note that review in this Court by means of a writ of certiorari is not a matter of right, but of judicial discretion. The primary concern of the Supreme Court is not to correct errors in lower court decisions, but to decide cases presenting issues of importance beyond the particular facts and parties involved. The Court grants and hears argument in only about 1% of the cases that are filed each Term. The vast majority of petitions are simply denied by the Court without comment or explanation. The denial of a petition for a writ of certiorari signifies only that the Court has chosen not to accept the case for review and does not express the Court's view of the merits of the case.

Every petitioner for a writ of certiorari is advised to read carefully the *Considerations Governing Review on Certiorari* set forth in Rule 10. Important considerations for accepting a case for review include the existence of a conflict between the decision of which review is sought and a decision of another appellate court on the same issue. An important function of the Supreme Court is to resolve disagreements among lower courts about specific legal questions. Another consideration is the importance to the public of the issue.

III. The Time for Filing

You must file your petition for a writ of certiorari within 90 days from the date of the entry of the final judgment in the United States court of appeals or highest state appellate court or 90 days from the denial of a timely filed petition for rehearing. The issuance of a mandate or remittitur after judgment has been entered has no bearing on the computation of time and does not extend the time for filing. See Rules 13.1 and decision could be had denied discretionary review, a copy of that order should follow. If an order denying a timely filed petition for rehearing starts the running of the time for filing a petition for a writ of certiorari pursuant to Rule 13.3, a copy of the order should be appended next.

As an example, if the state trial court ruled against you, the intermediate court of appeals affirmed the decision of the trial court, the state supreme court denied discretionary review and then denied a timely petition for rehearing, the appendices should appear in the following order:

Appendix A   Decision of State Court of Appeals

Appendix B   Decision of State Trial Court

Appendix C   Decision of State Supreme Court Denying Review

Appendix D   Order of State Supreme Court Denying Rehearing

VIII. Table of Authorities

On the page provided, list the cases, statutes, treatises, and articles that you reference in your petition, and the page number of your petition where each authority appears.

IX. Opinions Below

In the space provided, indicate whether the opinions of the lower courts in your case have been published, and if so, the citation for the opinion below. For example, opinions of the United States courts of appeals are published in the Federal Reporter. If the opinion in your case appears at page 100 of volume 30 of the Federal Reporter, Third Series, indicate that the opinion is reported at 30 F. 3d 100. If the opinion has been designated for publication but has not yet been published, check the appropriate space. Also indicate where in the appendix each decision, reported or unreported, appears.

X. Jurisdiction

The purpose of the jurisdiction section of the petition is to establish the statutory source for the Court's jurisdiction and the dates that determine whether the petition is timely filed. The form sets out the pertinent statutes for federal and state cases. You need provide only the dates of the lower court decisions that establish the timeliness of the petition for a writ of certiorari. If an extension of time within which to file the petition for a writ of certiorari was granted, you must provide the requested information pertaining to the extension. If you seek to have the Court review a decision of a state court, you must provide the date the highest state court decided your case, either by ruling on the merits or denying discretionary review.

XI. Constitutional and Statutory Provisions Involved

Set out verbatim the constitutional provisions, treaties, statutes, ordinances and regulations involved in the case. If the provisions involved are lengthy, provide their citation and indicate where in the Appendix to the petition the text of the provisions appears.

XII. Statement of the Case

Provide a **concise** statement of the case containing the facts material to the consideration of the question(s) presented; you should summarize the relevant facts of the case and the proceedings that took place in the lower courts. You may need to attach additional pages, but the statement should be concise and limited to the relevant facts of the case.

XIII. Reasons for Granting the Petition

The purpose of this section of the petition is to explain to the Court why it should grant certiorari. It is important to read Rule 10 and address what compelling reasons exist for the exercise of the Court's discretionary jurisdiction. Try to show not only why the decision of the lower court may be erroneous, but the national importance of having the Supreme Court decide the question involved. It is important to show whether the decision of the court that decided your case is in conflict with the decisions of another appellate court; the importance of the case not only to you but to others similarly situated; and the ways the decision of the lower court in your case was erroneous. You will need to attach additional pages, but the reasons should be as concise as possible, consistent with the purpose of this section of the petition.

XIV. Conclusion

Enter your name and the date that you submit the petition.

XV. Proof of Service

You must serve a copy of your petition on counsel for respondent(s) as required by Rule 29. If you serve the petition by first-class mail or by third-party commercial carrier, you may use the enclosed proof of service form. If the United States or any department, office, agency, officer, or employee thereof is a party, you must serve the Solicitor General of the United States, Room 5614, Department of Justice, 950 Pennsylvania Ave., N.W., Washington, D. C. 20530–0001. The lower courts that ruled on your case are not parties and need not be served with a copy of the petition. The proof of service may be in the form of a declaration pursuant to 28 U. S. C. § 1746.

No. _____

_____

IN THE

SUPREME COURT OF THE UNITED STATES

_____

_____ — PETITIONER
(Your Name)

VS.

_____ — RESPONDENT(S)

MOTION FOR LEAVE TO PROCEED *IN FORMA PAUPERIS*

    The petitioner asks leave to file the attached petition for a writ of certiorari without prepayment of costs and to proceed *in forma pauperis*.

    [ ] Petitioner has previously been granted leave to proceed *in forma pauperis* in the following court(s):

_____

_____

    [ ] Petitioner has **not** previously been granted leave to proceed *in forma pauperis* in any other court.

Petitioner's affidavit or declaration in support of this motion is attached hereto.

_____
(Signature)

AFFIDAVIT OR DECLARATION
IN SUPPORT OF MOTION FOR LEAVE TO PROCEED *IN FORMA PAUPERIS*

I, _____ , am the petitioner in the above-entitled case.   In support of my motion to proceed *in forma pauperis*, I state that because of my poverty I am unable to pay the costs of this case or to give security therefor; and I believe I am entitled to redress.

1. For both you and your spouse estimate the average amount of money received from each of the following sources during the past 12 months.   Adjust any amount that was received weekly, biweekly, quarterly, semiannually, or annually to show the monthly rate.   Use gross amounts, that is, amounts before any deductions for taxes or otherwise.

Income source	Average monthly amount during the past 12 months		Amount expected next month	
	You	Spouse	You	Spouse
Employment	$_____	$_____	$_____	$_____
Self-employment	$_____	$_____	$_____	$_____
Income from real property (such as rental income)	$_____	$_____	$_____	$_____
Interest and dividends	$_____	$_____	$_____	$_____
Gifts	$_____	$_____	$_____	$_____
Alimony	$_____	$_____	$_____	$_____
Child Support	$_____	$_____	$_____	$_____
Retirement (such as social security, pensions, annuities, insurance)	$_____	$_____	$_____	$_____
Disability (such as social security, insurance payments)	$_____	$_____	$_____	$_____
Unemployment payments	$_____	$_____	$_____	$_____
Public-assistance (such as welfare)	$_____	$_____	$_____	$_____
Other (specify): _____	$_____	$_____	$_____	$_____
Total monthly income:	$_____	$_____	$_____	$_____

2. List your employment history for the past two years, most recent first. (Gross monthly pay is before taxes or other deductions.)

Employer	Address	Dates of Employment	Gross monthly pay
			$_____
			$_____
			$_____

3. List your spouse's employment history for the past two years, most recent employer first. (Gross monthly pay is before taxes or other deductions.)

Employer	Address	Dates of Employment	Gross monthly pay
			$_____
			$_____
			$_____

4. How much cash do you and your spouse have? $_____
Below, state any money you or your spouse have in bank accounts or in any other financial institution.

Financial institution	Type of account	Amount you have	Amount your spouse has
		$_____	$_____
		$_____	$_____
		$_____	$_____

5. List the assets, and their values, which you own or your spouse owns. Do not list clothing and ordinary household furnishings.

☐ Home
    Value _____

☐ Other real estate
    Value _____

☐ Motor Vehicle #1
    Year, make & model _____
    Value _____

☐ Motor Vehicle #2
    Year, make & model _____
    Value _____

☐ Other assets
    Description _____
    Value _____

	You	Your spouse
Transportation (not including motor vehicle payments)	$____	$____
Recreation, entertainment, newspapers, magazines, etc.	$____	$____

Insurance (not deducted from wages or included in mortgage payments)

	You	Your spouse
Homeowner's or renter's	$____	$____
Life	$____	$____
Health	$____	$____
Motor Vehicle	$____	$____
Other: _____	$____	$____

Taxes (not deducted from wages or included in mortgage payments)

	You	Your spouse
(specify): _____	$____	$____

Installment payments

	You	Your spouse
Motor Vehicle	$____	$____
Credit card(s)	$____	$____
Department store(s)	$____	$____
Other: _____	$____	$____

	You	Your spouse
Alimony, maintenance, and support paid to others	$____	$____
Regular expenses for operation of business, profession, or farm (attach detailed statement)	$____	$____
Other (specify): _____	$____	$____
Total monthly expenses:	$____	$____

9. Do you expect any major changes to your monthly income or expenses or in your assets or liabilities during the next 12 months?

☐ Yes   ☐ No   If yes, describe on an attached sheet.

10. Have you paid – or will you be paying – an attorney any money for services in connection with this case, including the completion of this form?   ☐ Yes   ☐ No

If yes, how much? _____

If yes, state the attorney's name, address, and telephone number:

11. Have you paid—or will you be paying—anyone other than an attorney (such as a paralegal or a typist) any money for services in connection with this case, including the completion of this form?

☐ Yes   ☐ No

If yes, how much? _____

If yes, state the person's name, address, and telephone number:

12. Provide any other information that will help explain why you cannot pay the costs of this case.

I declare under penalty of perjury that the foregoing is true and correct.

Executed on: _____ , 20___

_____
(Signature)

6. State every person, business, or organization owing you or your spouse money, and the amount owed.

Person owing you or your spouse money	Amount owed to you	Amount owed to your spouse
_____	$_____	$_____
_____	$_____	$_____
_____	$_____	$_____

7. State the persons who rely on you or your spouse for support.

Name	Relationship	Age
_____	_____	_____
_____	_____	_____
_____	_____	_____

8. Estimate the average monthly expenses of you and your family. Show separately the amounts paid by your spouse. Adjust any payments that are made weekly, biweekly, quarterly, or annually to show the monthly rate.

	You	Your spouse
Rent or home-mortgage payment (include lot rented for mobile home)	$_____	$_____
Are real estate taxes included? ☐ Yes ☐ No		
Is property insurance included? ☐ Yes ☐ No		
Utilities (electricity, heating fuel, water, sewer, and telephone)	$_____	$_____
Home maintenance (repairs and upkeep)	$_____	$_____
Food	$_____	$_____
Clothing	$_____	$_____
Laundry and dry-cleaning	$_____	$_____
Medical and dental expenses	$_____	$_____

Northern District for the u.s district court

Pro se appearance limitation

Duty to notify the clerk's office by letter, by internet/email notification, or though cm/efc of any change in mailing address, telephone number or email address. Parties pro se shall notify the clerk's office so informed which cause a delay or otherwise adversely affect the management of a judgement by default.

LR3: Division of court-Venue

The northern district of Georgia consists of four(4). Divisions as outlined and described in 28 U.S.C.-90. REFER TO lr App. A. I, FOR LIST IOF counties comprising each division.

Venue and transfer of Venue for civil Actions.

B(3). WHERE THE cause of action arose.

Any civil action brought in this district on the grounds that the cause of action arose here must be filed in a district of the district wherein the activity took place.

LR3.3 CERTIFICATE of interested persons and corporate disclosure statement.

LR3.3(2). A complete list of other persons, associations, firms, partnerships, or Corporations having either a financial interest in or other interest in or other interest which could be substantially affected by the outcome of this particular case.

No. _____

_____

IN THE

SUPREME COURT OF THE UNITED STATES

_____

_____ — PETITIONER
(Your Name)

vs.

_____ — RESPONDENT(S)

ON PETITION FOR A WRIT OF CERTIORARI TO

_____

(NAME OF COURT THAT LAST RULED ON MERITS OF YOUR CASE)

PETITION FOR WRIT OF CERTIORARI

_____

(Your Name)

_____

(Address)

_____

(City, State, Zip Code)

_____

(Phone Number)

IN THE

SUPREME COURT OF THE UNITED STATES

PETITION FOR WRIT OF CERTIORARI

Petitioner respectfully prays that a writ of certiorari issue to review the judgment below.

OPINIONS BELOW

[ ] For cases from **federal courts**:

The opinion of the United States court of appeals appears at Appendix _____ to the petition and is

[ ] reported at _____; or,
[ ] has been designated for publication but is not yet reported; or,
[ ] is unpublished.

The opinion of the United States district court appears at Appendix _____ to the petition and is

[ ] reported at _____; or,
[ ] has been designated for publication but is not yet reported; or,
[ ] is unpublished.

[ ] For cases from **state courts**:

The opinion of the highest state court to review the merits appears at Appendix _____ to the petition and is

[ ] reported at _____; or,
[ ] has been designated for publication but is not yet reported; or,
[ ] is unpublished.

The opinion of the _____ court appears at Appendix _____ to the petition and is

[ ] reported at _____; or,
[ ] has been designated for publication but is not yet reported; or,
[ ] is unpublished.

1.

JURISDICTION

[ ] For cases from **federal courts**:

The date on which the United States Court of Appeals decided my case was _____.

[ ] No petition for rehearing was timely filed in my case.

[ ] A timely petition for rehearing was denied by the United States Court of Appeals on the following date: _____, and a copy of the order denying rehearing appears at Appendix _____.

[ ] An extension of time to file the petition for a writ of certiorari was granted to and including _____ (date) on _____ (date) in Application No. ___ A_____.

The jurisdiction of this Court is invoked under 28 U. S. C. § 1254(1).

[ ] For cases from **state courts**:

The date on which the highest state court decided my case was _____. A copy of that decision appears at Appendix _____.

[ ] A timely petition for rehearing was thereafter denied on the following date: _____, and a copy of the order denying rehearing appears at Appendix _____.

[ ] An extension of time to file the petition for a writ of certiorari was granted to and including _____ (date) on _____ (date) in Application No. ___ A_____.

The jurisdiction of this Court is invoked under 28 U. S. C. § 1257(a).

69

United States District Court for the Northern
District of Ohio

Plaintiff,

vs.

CASE NO. _____

Judge _____

Defendant.

NOTICE OF APPEAL

Notice is hereby given that _____,
(here name all parties taking the appeal)

hereby appeal to the United States Court of Appeals for the Sixth Circuit from

_____

(the final judgment) (from an order (describing it))

entered in this action on the _____ day of _____ , _____ . .

(s) _____

Address:

Phone #: _____

Attorney for _____

6CA-3

UNITED STATES DISTRICT COURT

for the

_____ District of _____

_____ Division

Plaintiff(s) *(Write the full name of each plaintiff who is filing this complaint. If the names of all the plaintiffs cannot fit in the space above, please write "see attached" in the space and attach an additional page with the full list of names.)* -v- Defendant(s) *(Write the full name of each defendant who is being sued. If the names of all the defendants cannot fit in the space above, please write "see attached" in the space and attach an additional page with the full list of names.)*	)))))))))))))))

Case No. _____
(to be filled in by the Clerk's Office)

Jury Trial: *(check one)* ☐ Yes ☐ No

COMPLAINT FOR VIOLATION OF FAIR LABOR STANDARDS

I. **The Parties to This Complaint**

   A. **The Plaintiff(s)**

   Provide the information below for each plaintiff named in the complaint. Attach additional pages if needed.

   Name _____

   Street Address _____

   City and County _____

   State and Zip Code _____

   Telephone Number _____

   E-mail Address _____

   B. **The Defendant(s)**

   Provide the information below for each defendant named in the complaint, whether the defendant is an individual, a government agency, an organization, or a corporation. For an individual defendant, include the person's job or title *(if known)*. Attach additional pages if needed.

The address at which I am employed or was employed by the defendant(s) is

Name

Street Address

City and County

State and Zip Code

Telephone Number

II. Basis for Jurisdiction

This action is brought pursuant to *(check all that apply)*:

☐ Fair Labor Standards Act, as codified, 29 U.S.C. §§ 201 to 209.

☐ Relevant state law

☐ Relevant city or county law

III. Statement of Claim

State as briefly as possible the facts of your case. You may wish to include further details such as the names of other persons involved in the events giving rise to your claims. Do not cite any cases. If more than one claim is asserted, number each claim and write a short and plain statement of each claim in a separate paragraph. Attach additional pages if needed.

A. Nature of employer's business:

B. Dates of employment:

C. Employee's job title and a description of the kind of work done:

D. Rate, method, and frequency of wage payment:

E.   Number of hours actually worked each week in which a violation is claimed:

F.   Description of the alleged violation(s) *(check all that apply)*:

☐   Failure to pay the minimum wage *(explain)*

☐   Failure to pay required overtime *(explain)*

☐   Other violation(s) *(explain)*

G.   Date(s) of the alleged violation(s):

H.   Additional facts:

IV. **Relief**

State briefly and precisely what damages or other relief the plaintiff asks the court to order. Do not make legal arguments. Include any basis for claiming that the wrongs alleged are continuing at the present time. Include the amounts of any actual damages claimed for the acts alleged and the basis for these amounts. Include any punitive or exemplary damages claimed, the amounts, and the reasons you claim you are entitled to actual or punitive money damages.

V. **Certification and Closing**

Under Federal Rule of Civil Procedure 11, by signing below, I certify to the best of my knowledge, information, and belief that this complaint: (1) is not being presented for an improper purpose, such as to harass, cause unnecessary delay, or needlessly increase the cost of litigation; (2) is supported by existing law or by a nonfrivolous argument for extending, modifying, or reversing existing law; (3) the factual contentions have evidentiary support or, if specifically so identified, will likely have evidentiary support after a reasonable opportunity for further investigation or discovery; and (4) the complaint otherwise complies with the requirements of Rule 11.

A. **For Parties Without an Attorney**

I agree to provide the Clerk's Office with any changes to my address where case-related papers may be served. I understand that my failure to keep a current address on file with the Clerk's Office may result in the dismissal of my case.

Date of signing: _____

Signature of Plaintiff _____

Printed Name of Plaintiff _____

B. **For Attorneys**

Date of signing: _____

Signature of Attorney _____

Printed Name of Attorney _____

Bar Number _____

74

Name of Law Firm _____

Street Address _____

State and Zip Code _____

Telephone Number _____

E-mail Address _____

UNITED STATES DISTRICT COURT

for the

_____ District of _____

_____ Division

	)	Case No. _____
	)	*(to be filled in by the Clerk's Office)*
_____	)	
Plaintiff(s)	)	
(Write the full name of each plaintiff who is filing this complaint.	)	Jury Trial: *(check one)* ☐ Yes ☐ No
If the names of all the plaintiffs cannot fit in the space above,	)	
please write "see attached" in the space and attach an additional	)	
page with the full list of names.)	)	
-v-	)	
	)	
	)	
	)	
	)	
_____	)	
Defendant(s)	)	
(Write the full name of each defendant who is being sued. If the	)	
names of all the defendants cannot fit in the space above, please	)	
write "see attached" in the space and attach an additional page	)	
with the full list of names.)		

COMPLAINT FOR EMPLOYMENT DISCRIMINATION

I.   **The Parties to This Complaint**

    A.   **The Plaintiff(s)**

        Provide the information below for each plaintiff named in the complaint. Attach additional pages if needed.

            Name   _____

            Street Address   _____

            City and County   _____

            State and Zip Code _____

            Telephone Number _____

            E-mail Address   _____

    B.   **The Defendant(s)**

        Provide the information below for each defendant named in the complaint, whether the defendant is an individual, a government agency, an organization, or a corporation. For an individual defendant, include the person's job or title *(if known)*. Attach additional pages if needed.

76

Defendant No. 1

Name

Job or Title *(if known)*

Street Address

City and County

State and Zip Code

Telephone Number

E-mail Address *(if known)*

Defendant No. 2

Name

Job or Title *(if known)*

Street Address

City and County

State and Zip Code

Telephone Number

E-mail Address *(if known)*

Defendant No. 3

Name

Job or Title *(if known)*

Street Address

City and County

State and Zip Code

Telephone Number

E-mail Address *(if known)*

Defendant No. 4

Name

Job or Title *(if known)*

Street Address

City and County

State and Zip Code

Telephone Number

E-mail Address *(if known)*

C.   Place of Employment

The address at which I sought employment or was employed by the defendant(s) is

Name

Street Address

City and County

State and Zip Code

Telephone Number

II.   Basis for Jurisdiction

This action is brought for discrimination in employment pursuant to *(check all that apply)*:

☐   Title VII of the Civil Rights Act of 1964, as codified, 42 U.S.C. §§ 2000e to 2000e-17 (race, color, gender, religion, national origin).

(Note: In order to bring suit in federal district court under Title VII, you must first obtain a Notice of Right to Sue letter from the Equal Employment Opportunity Commission.)

☐   Age Discrimination in Employment Act of 1967, as codified, 29 U.S.C. §§ 621 to 634.

(Note: In order to bring suit in federal district court under the Age Discrimination in Employment Act, you must first file a charge with the Equal Employment Opportunity Commission.)

☐   Americans with Disabilities Act of 1990, as codified, 42 U.S.C. §§ 12112 to 12117.

(Note: In order to bring suit in federal district court under the Americans with Disabilities Act, you must first obtain a Notice of Right to Sue letter from the Equal Employment Opportunity Commission.)

☐   Other federal law *(specify the federal law)*:

☐   Relevant state law *(specify, if known)*:

☐   Relevant city or county law *(specify, if known)*:

III. Statement of Claim

Write a short and plain statement of the claim. Do not make legal arguments. State as briefly as possible the facts showing that each plaintiff is entitled to the damages or other relief sought. State how each defendant was involved and what each defendant did that caused the plaintiff harm or violated the plaintiff's rights, including the dates and places of that involvement or conduct. If more than one claim is asserted, number each claim and write a short and plain statement of each claim in a separate paragraph. Attach additional pages if needed.

A. The discriminatory conduct of which I complain in this action includes *(check all that apply)*:

☐ Failure to hire me.

☐ Termination of my employment.

☐ Failure to promote me.

☐ Failure to accommodate my disability.

☐ Unequal terms and conditions of my employment.

☐ Retaliation.

☐ Other acts *(specify)*: _____

(Note: Only those grounds raised in the charge filed with the Equal Employment Opportunity Commission can be considered by the federal district court under the federal employment discrimination statutes.)

B. It is my best recollection that the alleged discriminatory acts occurred on date(s)

_____

C. I believe that defendant(s) *(check one)*:

☐ is/are still committing these acts against me.

☐ is/are not still committing these acts against me.

D. Defendant(s) discriminated against me based on my *(check all that apply and explain)*:

☐ race _____

☐ color _____

☐ gender/sex _____

☐ religion _____

☐ national origin _____

☐ age *(year of birth)* _____ *(only when asserting a claim of age discrimination.)*

☐ disability or perceived disability *(specify disability)*

_____

E. The facts of my case are as follows. Attach additional pages if needed.

(Note: As additional support for the facts of your claim, you may attach to this complaint a copy of your charge filed with the Equal Employment Opportunity Commission, or the charge filed with the relevant state or city human rights division.)

IV.   Exhaustion of Federal Administrative Remedies

A.   It is my best recollection that I filed a charge with the Equal Employment Opportunity Commission or my Equal Employment Opportunity counselor regarding the defendant's alleged discriminatory conduct on *(date)*

B.   The Equal Employment Opportunity Commission *(check one)*:

☐   has not issued a Notice of Right to Sue letter.

☐   issued a Notice of Right to Sue letter, which I received on *(date)* _____ .

(Note: Attach a copy of the Notice of Right to Sue letter from the Equal Employment Opportunity Commission to this complaint.)

C.   Only litigants alleging age discrimination must answer this question.

Since filing my charge of age discrimination with the Equal Employment Opportunity Commission regarding the defendant's alleged discriminatory conduct *(check one)*:

☐   60 days or more have elapsed.

☐   less than 60 days have elapsed.

V.   Relief

State briefly and precisely what damages or other relief the plaintiff asks the court to order. Do not make legal arguments. Include any basis for claiming that the wrongs alleged are continuing at the present time. Include the amounts of any actual damages claimed for the acts alleged and the basis for these amounts. Include any punitive or exemplary damages claimed, the amounts, and the reasons you claim you are entitled to actual or punitive money damages.

VI. Certification and Closing

Under Federal Rule of Civil Procedure 11, by signing below, I certify to the best of my knowledge, information, and belief that this complaint: (1) is not being presented for an improper purpose, such as to harass, cause unnecessary delay, or needlessly increase the cost of litigation; (2) is supported by existing law or by a nonfrivolous argument for extending, modifying, or reversing existing law; (3) the factual contentions have evidentiary support or, if specifically so identified, will likely have evidentiary support after a reasonable opportunity for further investigation or discovery; and (4) the complaint otherwise complies with the requirements of Rule 11.

A. **For Parties Without an Attorney**

I agree to provide the Clerk's Office with any changes to my address where case–related papers may be served. I understand that my failure to keep a current address on file with the Clerk's Office may result in the dismissal of my case.

Date of signing: _____

Signature of Plaintiff _____

Printed Name of Plaintiff _____

B. **For Attorneys**

Date of signing: _____

Signature of Attorney _____

Printed Name of Attorney _____

Bar Number _____

Name of Law Firm _____

Street Address _____

State and Zip Code _____

Telephone Number _____

E-mail Address _____

UNITED STATES DISTRICT COURT

for the

District of

Division

<table>
<tr><td></td><td>)</td><td>Case No. _____</td></tr>
<tr><td></td><td>)</td><td></td></tr>
<tr><td></td><td>)</td><td>(to be filled in by the Clerk's Office)</td></tr>
<tr><td>_____
Plaintiff(s)
(Write the full name of each plaintiff who is filing this complaint.
If the names of all the plaintiffs cannot fit in the space above,
please write "see attached" in the space and attach an additional
page with the full list of names.)
-v-</td><td>)
)
)
)
)
)
)</td><td></td></tr>
<tr><td></td><td>)</td><td>Jury Trial: (check one) ☐ Yes ☐ No</td></tr>
<tr><td>_____
Defendant(s)
(Write the full name of each defendant who is being sued. If the
names of all the defendants cannot fit in the space above, please
write "see attached" in the space and attach an additional page
with the full list of names.)</td><td>)
)
)
)
)
)
)
)
)</td><td></td></tr>
</table>

COMPLAINT FOR A CIVIL CASE

I.   The Parties to This Complaint

   A.   The Plaintiff(s)

   Provide the information below for each plaintiff named in the complaint. Attach additional pages if needed.

Name	_____
Street Address	_____
City and County	_____
State and Zip Code	_____
Telephone Number	_____
E-mail Address	_____

   B.   The Defendant(s)

   Provide the information below for each defendant named in the complaint, whether the defendant is an individual, a government agency, an organization, or a corporation. For an individual defendant, include the person's job or title *(if known)*. Attach additional pages if needed.

Defendant No. 1

    Name _____

    Job or Title *(if known)* _____

    Street Address _____

    City and County _____

    State and Zip Code _____

    Telephone Number _____

    E-mail Address *(if known)* _____

Defendant No. 2

    Name _____

    Job or Title *(if known)* _____

    Street Address _____

    City and County _____

    State and Zip Code _____

    Telephone Number _____

    E-mail Address *(if known)* _____

Defendant No. 3

    Name _____

    Job or Title *(if known)* _____

    Street Address _____

    City and County _____

    State and Zip Code _____

    Telephone Number _____

    E-mail Address *(if known)* _____

Defendant No. 4

    Name _____

    Job or Title *(if known)* _____

    Street Address _____

    City and County _____

    State and Zip Code _____

    Telephone Number _____

    E-mail Address *(if known)* _____

II.   Basis for Jurisdiction

Federal courts are courts of limited jurisdiction (limited power). Generally, only two types of cases can be heard in federal court: cases involving a federal question and cases involving diversity of citizenship of the parties. Under 28 U.S.C. § 1331, a case arising under the United States Constitution or federal laws or treaties is a federal question case. Under 28 U.S.C. § 1332, a case in which a citizen of one State sues a citizen of another State or nation and the amount at stake is more than $75,000 is a diversity of citizenship case. In a diversity of citizenship case, no defendant may be a citizen of the same State as any plaintiff.

What is the basis for federal court jurisdiction? *(check all that apply)*

☐ Federal question   ☐ Diversity of citizenship

Fill out the paragraphs in this section that apply to this case.

A.   If the Basis for Jurisdiction Is a Federal Question

List the specific federal statutes, federal treaties, and/or provisions of the United States Constitution that are at issue in this case.

B.   If the Basis for Jurisdiction Is Diversity of Citizenship

1.   The Plaintiff(s)

    a.   If the plaintiff is an individual

        The plaintiff, *(name)* _____ , is a citizen of the
        State of *(name)* _____ .

    b.   If the plaintiff is a corporation

        The plaintiff, *(name)* _____ , is incorporated
        under the laws of the State of *(name)* _____
        and has its principal place of business in the State of *(name)*
        _____ .

    (If more than one plaintiff is named in the complaint, attach an additional page providing the same information for each additional plaintiff.)

2.   The Defendant(s)

    a.   If the defendant is an individual

        The defendant, *(name)* _____ , is a citizen of
        the State of *(name)* _____ . Or is a citizen of
        (foreign nation) _____ .

84

b.   If the defendant is a corporation

The defendant, *(name)* _____ , is incorporated under

the laws of the State of *(name)* _____ , and has its

principal place of business in the State of *(name)* _____ .

Or is incorporated under the laws of *(foreign nation)* _____ ,

and has its principal place of business in *(name)* _____ .

(If more than one defendant is named in the complaint, attach an additional page providing the same information for each additional defendant.)

3.   The Amount in Controversy

The amount in controversy–the amount the plaintiff claims the defendant owes or the amount at stake–is more than $75,000, not counting interest and costs of court, because *(explain)*:

III.   Statement of Claim

Write a short and plain statement of the claim. Do not make legal arguments. State as briefly as possible the facts showing that each plaintiff is entitled to the damages or other relief sought. State how each defendant was involved and what each defendant did that caused the plaintiff harm or violated the plaintiff's rights, including the dates and places of that involvement or conduct. If more than one claim is asserted, number each claim and write a short and plain statement of each claim in a separate paragraph. Attach additional pages if needed.

IV.   Relief

State briefly and precisely what damages or other relief the plaintiff asks the court to order. Do not make legal arguments. Include any basis for claiming that the wrongs alleged are continuing at the present time. Include the amounts of any actual damages claimed for the acts alleged and the basis for these amounts. Include any punitive or exemplary damages claimed, the amounts, and the reasons you claim you are entitled to actual or punitive money damages.

V.   Certification and Closing

Under Federal Rule of Civil Procedure 11, by signing below, I certify to the best of my knowledge, information, and belief that this complaint: (1) is not being presented for an improper purpose, such as to harass, cause unnecessary delay, or needlessly increase the cost of litigation; (2) is supported by existing law or by a nonfrivolous argument for extending, modifying, or reversing existing law; (3) the factual contentions have evidentiary support or, if specifically so identified, will likely have evidentiary support after a reasonable opportunity for further investigation or discovery; and (4) the complaint otherwise complies with the requirements of Rule 11.

A.   For Parties Without an Attorney

I agree to provide the Clerk's Office with any changes to my address where case–related papers may be served. I understand that my failure to keep a current address on file with the Clerk's Office may result in the dismissal of my case.

Date of signing: _____

Signature of Plaintiff   _____
Printed Name of Plaintiff   _____

B.   For Attorneys

Date of signing: _____

Signature of Attorney   _____
Printed Name of Attorney   _____
Bar Number   _____
Name of Law Firm   _____
Street Address   _____
State and Zip Code   _____
Telephone Number   _____
E-mail Address   _____

UNITED STATES DISTRICT COURT
for the

_____	)
Plaintiff	)
v.	) Civil Action No.
_____	)
Defendant	)

SUMMONS IN A CIVIL ACTION

To: *(Defendant's name and address)*

A lawsuit has been filed against you.

Within 21 days after service of this summons on you (not counting the day you received it) — or 60 days if you are the United States or a United States agency, or an officer or employee of the United States described in Fed. R. Civ. P. 12 (a)(2) or (3) — you must serve on the plaintiff an answer to the attached complaint or a motion under Rule 12 of the Federal Rules of Civil Procedure. The answer or motion must be served on the plaintiff or plaintiff's attorney, whose name and address are:

If you fail to respond, judgment by default will be entered against you for the relief demanded in the complaint. You also must file your answer or motion with the court.

SANDY OPACICH, CLERK OF COURT

Date: _____

_____
Signature of Clerk or Deputy Clerk

UNITED STATES DISTRICT COURT
for the

_____)	
Plaintiff)	
v.)	Civil Action No.
_____)	
Defendant)	

NOTICE OF A LAWSUIT AND REQUEST TO WAIVE SERVICE OF A SUMMONS

To: _____
_____(Name of the defendant or - if the defendant is a corporation, partnership, or association - an officer or agent authorized to receive service)

Why are you getting this?

A lawsuit has been filed against you, or the entity you represent, in this court under the number shown above. A copy of the complaint is attached.

This is not a summons, or an official notice from the court. It is a request that, to avoid expenses, you waive formal service of a summons by signing and returning the enclosed waiver. To avoid these expenses, you must return the signed waiver within _____ days *(give at least 30 days, or at least 60 days if the defendant is outside any judicial district of the United States)* from the date shown below, which is the date this notice was sent. Two copies of the waiver form are enclosed, along with a stamped, self-addressed envelope or other prepaid means for returning one copy. You may keep the other copy.

What happens next?

If you return the signed waiver, I will file it with the court. The action will then proceed as if you had been served on the date the waiver is filed, but no summons will be served on you and you will have 60 days from the date this notice is sent (see the date below) to answer the complaint (or 90 days if this notice is sent to you outside any judicial district of the United States).

If you do not return the signed waiver within the time indicated, I will arrange to have the summons and complaint served on you. And I will ask the court to require you, or the entity you represent, to pay the expenses of making service.

Please read the enclosed statement about the duty to avoid unnecessary expenses.

I certify that this request is being sent to you on the date below.

Date: _____

_____
Signature of the attorney or unrepresented party

_____
Printed name
.

_____
Address

_____
E-mail address

_____
Telephone number

Civil Action No.

This summons for *(name of individual and title, if any)*

was received by me on *(date)*

☐ I personally served the summons on the individual at *(place)*

on *(date)* ; or

☐ I left the summons at the individual's residence or usual place of abode with *(name)*

, a person of suitable age and discretion who resides there,

on *(date)* , and mailed a copy to the individual's last known address; or

☐ I served the summons on *(name of individual)* , who is

designated by law to accept service of process on behalf of *(name of organization)*

on *(date)* ; or

☐ I returned the summons unexecuted because ; or

☐ Other *(specify):*

My fees are $ for travel and $ for services, for a total of $ 0.00

I declare under penalty of perjury that this information is true.

Date:

_____
Server's signature

_____
Printed name and title

_____
Server's address.

Additional information regarding attempted service, etc:

UNITED STATES DISTRICT COURT
for the

_____)
Plaintiff/Petitioner)
v.)   Civil Action No.
_____)
Defendant/Respondent)

APPLICATION TO PROCEED IN DISTRICT COURT WITHOUT PREPAYING FEES OR COSTS
(Long Form)

Affidavit in Support of the Application

I am a plaintiff or petitioner in this case and declare
that I am unable to pay the costs of these proceedings
and that I am entitled to the relief requested. I declare
under penalty of perjury that the information below is
true and understand that a false statement may result in
a dismissal of my claims.

Signed: _____

Instructions

Complete all questions in this application and then sign it.
Do not leave any blanks: if the answer to a question is "0,"
"none," or "not applicable (N/A)," write that response. If
you need more space to answer a question or to explain your
answer, attach a separate sheet of paper identified with your
name, your case's docket number, and the question number.

Date: _____

1. For both you and your spouse estimate the average amount of money received from each of the following
    sources during the past 12 months. Adjust any amount that was received weekly, biweekly, quarterly,
    semiannually, or annually to show the monthly rate. Use gross amounts, that is, amounts before any deductions
    for taxes or otherwise.

Income source	Average monthly income amount during the past 12 months		Income amount expected next month	
	You	Spouse	You	Spouse
Employment	$	$	$	$
Self-employment	$	$	$	$
Income from real property (such as rental income)	$	$	$	$
Interest and dividends	$	$	$	$
Gifts	$	$	$	$
Alimony	$	$	$	$
Child support	$	$	$	$

Retirement *(such as social security, pensions, annuities, insurance)*	$	$	$	$
Disability *(such as social security, insurance payments)*	$	$	$	$
Unemployment payments	$	$	$	$
Public-assistance *(such as welfare)*	$	$	$	$
Other *(specify):*	$	$	$	$
Total monthly income:	$ 0.00	$ 0.00	$ 0.00	$ 0.00

2.   List your employment history for the past two years, most recent employer first. *(Gross monthly pay is before taxes or other deductions.)*

Employer	Address	Dates of employment	Gross monthly pay
			$
			$

3.   List your spouse's employment history for the past two years, most recent employer first. *(Gross monthly pay is before taxes or other deductions.)*

Employer	Address	Dates of employment	Gross monthly pay
			$
			$
			$

4.   How much cash do you and your spouse have? $ _____

Below, state any money you or your spouse have in bank accounts or in any other financial institution.

Financial institution	Type of account	Amount you have	Amount your spouse has
		$	$
		$	$
		$	$

If you are a prisoner, you must attach a statement certified by the appropriate institutional officer showing all receipts, expenditures, and balances during the last six months in your institutional accounts. If you have multiple accounts, perhaps because you have been in multiple institutions, attach one certified statement of each account.

5. List the assets, and their values, which you own or your spouse owns. Do not list clothing and ordinary household furnishings.

Assets owned by you or your spouse	
Home *(Value)*	$
Other real estate *(Value)*	$
Motor vehicle #*1 (Value)*	$
Make and year:	
Model:	
Registration #:	
Motor vehicle #*2 (Value)*	$
Make and year:	
Model:	
Registration #:	
Other assets *(Value)*	$
Other assets *(Value)*	$

6. State every person, business, or organization owing you or your spouse money, and the amount owed.

Person owing you or your spouse money	Amount owed to you	Amount owed to your spouse
	$	$
	$	$
	$	$

7. State the persons who rely on you or your spouse for support.

Name (or, if under 18, initials only)	Relationship	Age

8. Estimate the average monthly expenses of you and your family. Show separately the amounts paid by your spouse. Adjust any payments that are made weekly, biweekly, quarterly, semiannually, or annually to show the monthly rate.

	You	Your spouse
Rent or home-mortgage payment *(including lot rented for mobile home)* Are real estate taxes included?　☐ Yes　☐ No Is property insurance included?　☐ Yes　☐ No	$	$
Utilities *(electricity, heating fuel, water, sewer, and telephone)*	$	$
Home maintenance *(repairs and upkeep)*	$	$
Food	$	$
Clothing	$	$
Laundry and dry-cleaning	$	$
Medical and dental expenses	$	$
Transportation *(not including motor vehicle payments)*	$	$
Recreation, entertainment, newspapers, magazines, etc.	$	$
Insurance *(not deducted from wages or included in mortgage payments)*		
Homeowner's or renter's:	$	$
Life:	$	$
Health:	$	$
Motor vehicle:	$	$
Other:	$	$
Taxes *(not deducted from wages or included in mortgage payments) (specify):*	$	$
Installment payments		
Motor vehicle:	$	$
Credit card *(name):*	$	$
Department store *(name):*	$	$
Other:	$	$
Alimony, maintenance, and support paid to others	$	$

Regular expenses for operation of business, profession, or farm *(attach detailed statement)*	$		$	
Other *(specify)*:	$		$	
Total monthly expenses:	$	0.00	$	0.00

9. Do you expect any major changes to your monthly income or expenses or in your assets or liabilities during the next 12 months?

    ❐ Yes   ❐ No   If yes, describe on an attached sheet.

10. Have you spent — or will you be spending — any money for expenses or attorney fees in conjunction with this lawsuit?   ❐ Yes ❐ No

    If yes, how much? $

11. Provide any other information that will help explain why you cannot pay the costs of these proceedings.

12. Identify the city and state of your legal residence.

    Your daytime phone number:

    Your age: Your years of schooling:

UNITED STATES DISTRICT COURT

for the

_____ District of _____

_____ Division

	)	Case No. _____
	)	_(to be filled in by the Clerk's Office)_
Plaintiff(s)	)	
(Write the full name of each plaintiff who is filing this complaint.	)	Jury Trial: _(check one)_ ☐ Yes ☐ No
If the names of all the plaintiffs cannot fit in the space above,	)	
please write "see attached" in the space and attach an additional	)	
page with the full list of names.)	)	
-v-	)	
	)	
	)	
	)	
	)	
Defendant(s)	)	
(Write the full name of each defendant who is being sued. If the	)	
names of all the defendants cannot fit in the space above, please	)	
write "see attached" in the space and attach an additional page		
with the full list of names. Do not include addresses here.)		

COMPLAINT FOR VIOLATION OF CIVIL RIGHTS
(Non-Prisoner Complaint)

NOTICE

Federal Rules of Civil Procedure 5.2 addresses the privacy and security concerns resulting from public access to electronic court files. Under this rule, papers filed with the court should *not* contain: an individual's full social security number or full birth date; the full name of a person known to be a minor; or a complete financial account number. A filing may include *only*: the last four digits of a social security number; the year of an individual's birth; a minor's initials; and the last four digits of a financial account number.

Except as noted in this form, plaintiff need not send exhibits, affidavits, grievance or witness statements, or any other materials to the Clerk's Office with this complaint.

In order for your complaint to be filed, it must be accompanied by the filing fee or an application to proceed in forma pauperis.

I. The Parties to This Complaint

A. The Plaintiff(s)

Provide the information below for each plaintiff named in the complaint. Attach additional pages if needed.

Name _____

Address _____

_____

| | City | State | Zip Code |

County _____

Telephone Number _____

E-Mail Address _____

B. The Defendant(s)

Provide the information below for each defendant named in the complaint, whether the defendant is an individual, a government agency, an organization, or a corporation. For an individual defendant, include the person's job or title (if known) and check whether you are bringing this complaint against them in their individual capacity or official capacity, or both. Attach additional pages if needed.

Defendant No. 1

Name _____

Job or Title *(if known)* _____

Address _____

| | City | State | Zip Code |

County _____

Telephone Number _____

E-Mail Address *(if known)* _____

☐ Individual capacity ☐ Official capacity

Defendant No. 2

Name _____

Job or Title *(if known)* _____

Address _____

| | City | State | Zip Code |

County _____

Telephone Number _____

E-Mail Address *(if known)* _____

☐ Individual capacity ☐ Official capacity

96

Defendant No. 3
  Name
  Job or Title *(if known)*
  Address

	City	State	Zip Code

  County
  Telephone Number
  E-Mail Address *(if known)*

  ☐ Individual capacity　　☐ Official capacity

Defendant No. 4
  Name
  Job or Title *(if known)*
  Address

	City	State	Zip Code

  County
  Telephone Number
  E-Mail Address *(if known)*

  ☐ Individual capacity　　☐ Official capacity

II.　Basis for Jurisdiction

Under 42 U.S.C. § 1983, you may sue state or local officials for the "deprivation of any rights, privileges, or immunities secured by the Constitution and [federal laws]." Under *Bivens v. Six Unknown Named Agents of Federal Bureau of Narcotics, 403 U.S. 388 (1971)*, you may sue federal officials for the violation of certain constitutional rights.

A.　Are you bringing suit against *(check all that apply)*:

　　☐ Federal officials (a *Bivens* claim)

　　☐ State or local officials (a § 1983 claim)

B.　Section 1983 allows claims alleging the "deprivation of any rights, privileges, or immunities secured by the Constitution and [federal laws]." 42 U.S.C. § 1983. If you are suing under section 1983, what federal constitutional or statutory right(s) do you claim is/are being violated by state or local officials?

C.　Plaintiffs suing under *Bivens* may only recover for the violation of certain constitutional rights. If you are suing under *Bivens*, what constitutional right(s) do you claim is/are being violated by federal officials?

97

D.   Section 1983 allows defendants to be found liable only when they have acted "under color of any statute, ordinance, regulation, custom, or usage, of any State or Territory or the District of Columbia." 42 U.S.C. § 1983. If you are suing under section 1983, explain how each defendant acted under color of state or local law. If you are suing under *Bivens*, explain how each defendant acted under color of federal law. Attach additional pages if needed.

III.   Statement of Claim

State as briefly as possible the facts of your case. Describe how each defendant was personally involved in the alleged wrongful action, along with the dates and locations of all relevant events. You may wish to include further details such as the names of other persons involved in the events giving rise to your claims. Do not cite any cases or statutes. If more than one claim is asserted, number each claim and write a short and plain statement of each claim in a separate paragraph. Attach additional pages if needed.

A.   Where did the events giving rise to your claim(s) occur?

B.   What date and approximate time did the events giving rise to your claim(s) occur?

C.   What are the facts underlying your claim(s)? *(For example: What happened to you? Who did what? Was anyone else involved? Who else saw what happened?)*

IV.   **Injuries**

If you sustained injuries related to the events alleged above, describe your injuries and state what medical treatment, if any, you required and did or did not receive.

V.   **Relief**

State briefly what you want the court to do for you. Make no legal arguments. Do not cite any cases or statutes. If requesting money damages, include the amounts of any actual damages and/or punitive damages claimed for the acts alleged. Explain the basis for these claims.

VI.   Certification and Closing

Under Federal Rule of Civil Procedure 11, by signing below, I certify to the best of my knowledge, information, and belief that this complaint: (1) is not being presented for an improper purpose, such as to harass, cause unnecessary delay, or needlessly increase the cost of litigation; (2) is supported by existing law or by a nonfrivolous argument for extending, modifying, or reversing existing law; (3) the factual contentions have evidentiary support or, if specifically so identified, will likely have evidentiary support after a reasonable opportunity for further investigation or discovery; and (4) the complaint otherwise complies with the requirements of Rule 11.

A.   For Parties Without an Attorney

I agree to provide the Clerk's Office with any changes to my address where case–related papers may be served. I understand that my failure to keep a current address on file with the Clerk's Office may result in the dismissal of my case.

Date of signing: _____

Signature of Plaintiff _____

Printed Name of Plaintiff _____

B.   For Attorneys

Date of signing: _____

Signature of Attorney _____

Printed Name of Attorney _____

Bar Number _____

Name of Law Firm _____

Address _____

	City	State	Zip Code

Telephone Number _____

E-mail Address _____

UNITED STATES DISTRICT COURT
for the

_____)	
Plaintiff)	
v.)	Civil Action No.
_____)	
Defendant)	

SUBPOENA TO APPEAR AND TESTIFY
AT A HEARING OR TRIAL IN A CIVIL ACTION

To:

YOU ARE COMMANDED to appear in the United States district court at the time, date, and place set forth below to testify at a hearing or trial in this civil action. When you arrive, you must remain at the court until the judge or a court officer allows you to leave. If you are an organization that is *not* a party in this case, you must designate one or more officers, directors, or managing agents, or designate other persons who consent to testify on your behalf about the following matters, or those set forth in an attachment:

Place:	Courtroom No.:
	Date and Time:

You must also bring with you the following documents, electronically stored information, or objects *(blank if not applicable)*:

The provisions of Fed. R. Civ. P. 45(c), relating to your protection as a person subject to a subpoena, and Fed. R. Civ. P. 45 (d) and (e), relating to your duty to respond to this subpoena and the potential consequences of not doing so, are attached.

Date: _____

        SANDY OPACICH, CLERK OF COURT

                            OR

_____   _____
  Signature of Clerk or Deputy Clerk   *Attorney's signature*

The name, address, e-mail, and telephone number of the attorney representing *(name of party)* _____
_____ , who issues or requests this subpoena, are:

CPSIA information can be obtained
at www.ICGtesting.com
Printed in the USA
BVHW031339020919
557356BV00009B/151/P

9 781728 322995